THE CONSUMER EDUCATION SERIES

A PLACE TO LIVE

GOVERNMENT SERVICES FOR CONSUMERS

THE TEEN-AGER AND HIS FAMILY

VIEWING YOUR CAREER

☐ CONSUMER PURCHASING

MAJORITY AT 18

HEALTH AND LEISURE

CAR PURCHASE AND MAINTENANCE

DOLLAR POWER

CONSUMER PURCHASING

ROBERT W. RANDALL

MORRIS GALL, SERIES EDITOR

Pendulum Press, Inc.

West Haven, Connecticut   El Monte, California

First Printing. . . . . . .November 1973
Second Printing. . . . . .September 1974

ISBN 0-88301-113-1 *Complete Set*
      0-88301-118-2 *This Volume*

Library of Congress Catalog Card Number 73-83978

Published by
Pendulum Press, Inc
An Academic Industries, Inc. Company
The Academic Building
Saw Mill Road
West Haven, Connecticut 06516

Printed in the United States of America

CONTENTS

INTRODUCTION

The ancient Romans coined the expression *caveat emptor,* or "let the buyer beware." Two thousand years and many economic, political, and social revolutions later, the warning is as pertinent as ever. Today's buyer is confused by a multiplicity of products and by the welter of advertising claims surrounding him. It is a mistake to think anyone can buy wisely or get his moneysworth without effort.

But effort alone will not suffice. None of us has either the know-how or the time to analyze the goods and services we purchase with our hard-earned dollars. Yet, every day, as we enter the marketplace—not only our dollars but our health and our very lives are at stake.

Fortunately there are sources of information and many safeguards—both voluntary and legal—to help the consumer get a fair deal. It is the purpose of this series to give the buyer—especially young consumers just entering the marketplace—the tools needed to get their moneysworth. This includes information on sources of help in making wise buying choices and the means available for remedying inequities when they occur.

Beyond that, the **Consumer Education Series** seeks to build attitudes about consumer problems that will have long-term influence on buying habits. This influence can exercise leverage on producers, sellers, and government to correct the abuses of which today's buyer is too often an innocent victim.

The Consumer Education Series focuses on nine specific areas of the marketplace. These are interrelated but each confronts the buyer with special problems calling for special information.

Each book seeks to develop in the student the disposition to take action as a consumer in his own interest. Whether it be to seek information or to prod producer, vendor, or government, a public consisting of well informed, alert, determined consumers *can* make a difference. That, at least, is the point of view from which these books are written.

In the long run, an intelligent body of consumers will secure a fair deal in the marketplace for themselves and others. They will protect their health and their lives. And they will serve to strengthen both the economy and the body politic. This is the rationale for the **Consumer Education Series**.

—Morris Gall

CHAPTER ONE
TRUTH-IN-LENDING

Americans use more credit than anyone else in the world. In fact, American consumers owe about $400 billion in credit, yet most Americans do not know what they pay for credit. A recent study of consumer credit found that less than one in five families knew what they were paying; most of them were paying three times what they believed. Younger credit users made more mistakes than older ones while most people falsely believed that all credit costs about the same.

Consider the possibilities open to a young consumer wishing to purchase a used car. The consumer has saved $500 and needs $1,000 more to buy the car he has in mind. He can obtain the $1,000 from three possible sources: the used car company, his savings and loan bank, or his uncle. The used car company suggests he borrow the $1,000 and pay back $1,100 in eleven monthly installments. The savings and loan bank enables him to borrow the $1,000 and pay back $1,100 one year later. His uncle loans him $1,000 less $100 charge in advance and wants him to pay the $1,000 in eleven monthly installments.

The uninformed consumer takes a quick look at the options and decides they all have about the same 10 percent interest rate. He chooses the used car company's offer, thereby making a mistake. Only the savings and loan bank enables him to have use of his money for a full year; the car company takes back part of his money the first month. On the average, the consumer had use of only half of the money for the year, and the true interest rate was about 18 percent; his uncle's interest rate was even higher. By charging the interest in advance, the consumer's uncle makes 20 percent from his loan—twice the rate of the savings and loan offer. Had the consumer realized the true interest rate of each option, he would have chosen wisely and borrowed from the savings and loan bank; but he was uninformed.

The need for the public to know the true cost of credit resulted in the Consumer Credit Protection Act of 1968, which included a law entitled Truth-in-Lending. As a result, shopping for credit has become less of a mystery: the price of the loan must be clearly stated; the lender must tell you the *finance charge*, the number of dollars you pay to borrow the money. More important, he must tell you the true annual percentage rate you pay for the money you borrow, because it is the only reliable way to measure one lender's charge against another's. The lower the interest rate, the less you pay for the loan. The law also makes the lender tell the borrower:

- —the date on which the finance charge begins
- —the number, amount, and due dates of payments
- —the total amount to be paid
- —the penalty for any delay in payment
- —a description of anything owned by the borrower held as security by the lender (when the borrower pays back the money on time, the security is returned.)
- —if the borrower has offered his home as security, he has the right to cancel the loan within three business days after the contract has been signed, and before

the money has been lent.

Installment credit was originally a service to the customer. More than one hundred years ago, Mr. Singer invented a sewing machine which could supply a way to produce clothing at low cost to every home. A great need existed, yet initial cost was too high for most people even though the machine would enable its owner to save money in the long run. Consequently, Mr. Singer developed installment payments and sold his sewing machine around the world; his grateful customers were happy to pay the cost of credit.

Today, the seller may make more money on finance charges than on outright sale of merchandise. The service of providing credit has become a profit-maker for the seller and an extra cost for the buyer. The seller may advertise his finance plans along with what he is selling; additional charges are made for "insurance" or "handling." Some people buy goods they do not need because they can buy them the easy way; in fact, the trend towards installment buying for all merchandise is growing. The National Consumer Finance Association predicts that all groups of Americans will increase their use of installment buying and that younger and poorer Americans will especially need installment buying to purchase items they think they need.

Recent studies by the Federal Trade Commission (FTC) show that 27 percent of retail sales are made using installment credit. However, for low income people the sales figure is 93 percent. Most of these sales to low income people seeking credit involves increased prices as well. For example, a clothes dryer bought by a dealer for $115, is made to sell for $150 in a regular store. In the low income installment market the dryer costs $300, plus the cost of credit. There are many other examples of products sold at very high prices to people who can least afford them.

COST OF CREDIT

THE KIND OF CREDIT	THE TRUE ANNUAL INTEREST RATE PER YEAR	RECOMMENDATION
1. College education loans that qualify for federal support	3%	By all means!
2. Other college education loans	7%	Designed for good students.
3. First mortgage home loans, monthly payment plan	8%	Good for most families with permanent, stable employment.
4. Home improvement loans from savings and loan associations and banks without security	11 to 13½%	High interest rates to be avoided except in cases of extreme need.
5. Credit union loans	12%	Often the cheapest and most satisfactory form of small loans.
6. Most credit cards and store plans	18%	Use it sparingly. Unless you pay bills promptly.
7. 30-day retail credit	None if paid in 30 days	Pay on time!
8. Car loans	9%—	Beware of the high cost of required insurance.
9. Appliance loans	18% and higher	Cash will usually buy it for 20% to 30% less.
10. Personal loans—confidential—no questions asked	30% and higher	Not recommended.
11. Loans from friends, relatives or employers	optional	Often leads to many problems.
12. Loan sharks	unlimited	Never.

Installment buying may cause legal problems for the buyer who is late in making payments. If the buyer fails to pay an installment when due the seller may seek a court decision to take back the merchandise. This is called *repossession;* the seller does not return any money. A court may also order the buyer's employer to make direct payment to the seller. Money is deducted from the buyer's paycheck until the purchase price and additional 10 percent charges are paid. This is a *garnishment*. There are varying state laws regulating the amount of a garnishment. As harsh and troublesome as court action might be, some installment sellers regard it as a normal part of their business.

Many Americans regard installment buying as a credit habit of the poor, yet the credit card is commonly used by people of higher economic standing. In fact, there were seventy million oil company cards in circulation in 1970, compared to twenty-three million in 1967. There are sixty-one million bank credit cards and eleven million airlines or entertainment club cards as well. Altogether there are nearly as many credit cards (200 million) as there are Americans. Here are the reasons for the growth of this kind of credit.

1. There is no need to carry a lot of cash. The danger of losing money or being robbed is lessened.
2. It is more convenient to write only one check, instead of many, to pay your bills.
3. The bill from the credit card company serves as a simple bookkeeping method that tells where your money is spent.
4. A card holder has available credit to take advantage of sales and thus save money.

When you use the card, you agree to the terms set forth by the issuing company even though no formal agreement has been signed. Read these items carefully and make sure all questions are answered before you use the card. Some companies can call for full payment at any time without notice, and may also have the right to take over the card holder's property to pay the debt. Moreover, the company may change the terms of the agreement at any time. Remember to destroy any card issued to you that you do not intend to use.

Establishing and maintaining a good credit rating is very important. How well you have met debts in the past helps determine your credit rating. One of the ironies of the American system of free enterprise is that many people who have always paid cash have no credit rating or a poor credit rating. The best way to establish credit is to open a small credit account and pay each installment promptly. If you go away, make the payments in advance; budget your credit carefully; choose the best service at the lowest cost. If a genuine emergency arises, discuss your problem frankly with your creditors. Try to arrange a new payment plan without penalty, however, if repossession is the only course, return the goods yourself. If you are unsure what to do, several services are available in most cities: the Consumer Credit Counseling Service, the National Consumer Finance Association, and the National Foundation for Consumer Credit. Establishing and maintaining credit enable you to remain independent and can help you meet opportunities or emergencies.

CHAPTER REVIEW

I. GAINING KNOWLEDGE

Find the meaning of each of these words and phrases. Use each in a sentence of your own.

competition	repossession
contract	security
credit bureau	Truth-in-Lending
garnish	

II. BUILDING SKILLS

You purchase a car for $2,000 on July 1 and pay $1,000 cash. You borrow $1,000 and agree to make monthly payments of $100 starting on August 1 and the last or eleventh payment the following June 1. What is your true interest rate? This is the formula used to determine the annual interest rate:

$$\text{Rate} = \frac{2\,PC}{A\,(N \text{ plus } 1)}$$

Legend: P = number of payments in one year
          C = finance charges
          A = loan
          N = number of installments

III. EXPLORING VALUES

Do you agree or disagree with the following? Why?

1. "Buy now, pay later" is always good advice.
2. When you lend a lot of money to a friend for several months, he should pay you interest.
3. Poor people should be restricted by law to the amount they may borrow.
4. All loaning of money for interest (profit) should be outlawed. Except for big purchases like a house or possibly a car, you shouldn't use credit.

IV. TAKING ACTION

1. Invite a finance officer from a local bank or loan company to speak to the class on loan policies.
2. Attend a small claims court session and sit in on a repossession or garnishment case.
3. Visit a local credit bureau and ask for a reference on yourself.
4. Collect pamphlets or contracts from credit unions, stores, local finance companies, and the Consumer Credit Counseling Service. Compare the cost of credit and debtor rights.

CHAPTER TWO
FOOD VALUE AND COST

Advertising is notorious for its ability to mislead the consumer. Many food product ads focus on making people popular rather than healthy. Food advertising has created a false picture of nutrition. In the United States today, over $70 a year is spent on advertising for each person. Much of the advertising is aimed at the uninformed, those consumers least able to make wise decisions. The reason for practically all food advertising is to sell goods, not to improve people's diets. Most food ads are made by the makers of coffee, breakfast foods, cookies, cake mixes, salad dressings, canned fruit drinks, chewing gum, soda-pop, desserts, beer, and cheese foods. All except the cheese have little or no natural vitamins, minerals, or body building proteins. Most of the energy in these heavily advertised foods is quickly used leaving the user in need of more energy.

Food-makers have nevertheless made many improvements in the past forty years. The possibilities for a healthy economical diet are greater now than ever. Competition has brought higher quality at a lower price. Since the 1920s frozen foods have made it possible to eat fresh vegetables throughout the year. Foods keep longer and are shipped more easily, there is a variety of foods to fit every taste, and boxed mixes and canned foods have reduced the preparation of meals to minutes. Food labels provide more and more information, yet most Americans have poor diets. Young people especially need nutritious food to gain full mental and physical maturity. The American food industry has provided the possibilities for a good diet. Because of the large profits in the sugar/starch foods, however, the food industry ads do not properly stress better meat, vegetables, fruit, milk, and grain products.

Of the top selling sixty brands of cereals, only nine have passing food value. Most cereals are inferior to much less expensive foods, such as breads, oatmeal, beans, rice, or corn. The energy supplied is of the short term variety: most of the protein is not available to the body; most vitamins and minerals are artificial additives to replace those lost in processing.

Each year the cereal industry sells about $700 million worth of packaged cereals and spends $75 million on advertising. Profits are very high. Bulk *wholesale* prices for corn and oats are about 2 cents per pound. The processed product may be close to $1 per pound. Yet the food value in the product is less than the original corn and oats. Obviously, most breakfast cereals are a poor buy. Rolled oats provide much more protein, energy value, minerals, and vitamins than most processed cold cereals. They are much more economical.

The addition of artificial *nutrients* to America's food supply has greatly improved our diet. Arletta M. Beloian, a government research *nutritionist,* found that the American diet varies from season to season. During the spring, vitamins A and C are below the minimum requirements for good health. During the summer the same is true for the mineral, calcium. Enrichment of white flour with artificial iron and calcium is suggested to solve the calcium problem. Most fruit drinks have improved their nutritional value by including artificial Vitamin C.

In the past thirty years the scarce Vitamin D has been added to milk, Vitamin A to margarine, and iodine to salt to help solve national dietary problems. Such artificially treated foods are called *fortified*. Foods in which the natural nutrients have been replaced by artificial nutrients are called *enriched*. Enriched foods must contain thiamine, riboflavin, niacin, and iron. The artificial variety adds 50 percent more thiamine to the nation's diet than would otherwise have been available. Processed foods that have been enriched with artificial nutrients are certainly preferable to those without fortification, but they are not as healthful as foods with natural nutrients.

The Food and Drug Administration (FDA) further states that there is no need for special diet *supplements* for most people. Most of the nutritional needs of Americans can be met by the readily available foods on the market. If a person follows a proper diet, most food supplements sold as pills, capsules, liquids, or powders have little value. The body passes off the vitamins and minerals it does not need. Much of the current demand for supplements is caused by the term "minimum daily requirement" (MDR). This term was used by the FDA thirty-five years ago but has become misleading. The FDA now uses the phrase, "recommended dietary allowance" (RDA).

The proper way to good health is to eat reasonable amounts of the four basic foods: 1) milk, 2) vegetables and fruit, 3) meat, 4) bread and cereals; to exercise and to keep well rested and clean.

The bread and cereal group includes all breads and cereals that are whole grain, enriched, or fortified. Breads, cooked cereals, cornmeal, crackers, flour, grits, spaghetti, rice, and rolled oats all provide food energy and some amounts of protein, iron, and the B vitamins. The necessary

FOLLOW THE FOOD GUIDE EVERY DAY

SOME for Everyone	**MILK GROUP** COUNT AS A SERVING 1 CUP ⊔ OF MILK Children under 9 Adults ⊔⊔ or more Children 9-12 ⊔⊔⊔ or more Pregnant Women ⊔⊔⊔ or more Teen-agers ⊔⊔⊔⊔ or more Nursing Mothers ⊔⊔⊔⊔ or more Cheese can be used for part of the MILK
2 or more Servings	**MEAT GROUP** COUNT AS A SERVING 2 OR 3 OUNCES OF COOKED LEAN MEAT, POULTRY, OR FISH—SUCH AS A Hamburger or a Chicken Leg or a Fish or 2 EGGS or 1 CUP COOKED DRY BEANS OR PEAS or 4 TABLESPOONS PEANUT BUTTER
4 or more Servings	**VEGETABLE-FRUIT GROUP** COUNT AS A SERVING ½ CUP (RAW OR COOKED) or 1 PORTION SUCH AS A Banana Potato Orange Spicy Tomato Sauce
4 or more Servings	**BREAD-CEREAL GROUP** (Whole Grain or Enriched) COUNT AS A SERVING 1 SLICE OF BREAD OR A CUPCAKE OR 1 OUNCE READY-TO-EAT CEREAL OR ½ CUP TO ¾ CUP COOKED CEREAL CORNMEAL, RICE, OR SPAGHETTI

Eat other foods as needed to round out the meals.

SOURCE: UNITED STATES DEPARTMENT OF AGRICULTURE, CONSUMER AND MARKETING SERVICE, AGRICULTURAL RESEARCH SERVICE, JULY 1966

intake of this group is rarely a problem. General Foods Corporation has recently developed a high protein pasta made from corn, soy beans, and wheat that is now being distributed through public food programs in American schools and hospitals and in Latin America. Tasteless fish flour has been added to white wheat flour to improve its protein content. It is this group, however, along with the less desirable sweet or fatty foods that often cause fat to form in the body. If you want to gain weight, eat an extra serving from this group and gain an extra hour's sleep per night. If you wish to lose weight, increase your daily exercise perhaps by walking to school, dancing, or playing basketball or ping pong. Decrease your food energy (calories) intake slightly by drinking non-fat milk. Avoid sweets.

In 1906, and again in 1938, Congress passed laws requiring standard labeling on foods. The government, however, does not require quality standards for packaged foods. Since people differ in their tastes and may prefer a variety of seasonings, the government asks for physical descriptions only. This allows the consumer to decide whether early, young, or mature peas are the best. Quality may be a matter of a personal judgment. You do not always have to pay the highest price to get what *you* consider to be the best buy.

Many people feel the labeling laws have not gone far enough. The FDA is considering laws which require complete nutritional information on the label. So many of the new easy-to-prepare foods lack food value, that Americans often lack a balanced diet and do not know it. Many foods are high in saturated fats and can cause physical conditions that bring on heart attacks. The FDA hopes that the information provided on the label will help Americans improve their diets. However, it is a difficult problem because nutritional values can be affected by harvesting and cooking methods, and by storage and handling.

The government has no power to change prices directly. In fact, the Federal Government has a responsibility to protect competition in America's market place. The government has the responsibility to ensure that the American citizen can buy safe, clean, pure, wholesome, and healthful products of his own choice. In 1966, the 89th Congress enacted the Fair Packaging and Labeling Act. All packaging in interstate commerce must be honestly and clearly labeled so that any shopper may easily get accurate information. The law does not allow the use of such misleading terms as "giant quart" or "jumbo pound." A jumbo pound has 16 ounces just like a "teeny pound." Some stores raise prices and then lower them. Sales that claim "cents-off" rarely reflect a savings over the regular price. Though the law is in effect, it is difficult to enforce. The consumer himself should report all violations to the FDA.

The Federal Government also has provided guidelines for cleanliness in the food industry. The FDA inspects food plants to see that the law is being obeyed. To be sure that food is clean and wholesome the FDA requires:

1. Properly constructed and screened buildings to protect the food from rodents, insects, and birds.
2. Equipment that can be thoroughly cleaned.
3. Employees who are clean in their dress, habits, and food-handling.
4. Storage that gives protection from spoilage or contamination (contact with poisons or impure substances).

Under the Federal Food Drug and Cosmetic Act (FDC), any food is considered impure if any part of it is impure or if it was prepared under unclean conditions. To prevent food from being declared impure, the FDA tries to inform businessmen about the law. The seizure of their products may cost businessmen many thousands of dollars. If the FDA proves in court that a producer is guilty of violating the law, he may be fined and/or sent to prison.

Ensuring clean food requires constant effort. The FDA has the power to bring violators to court, or recall impure food, or seize stocks of food. It may prevent further sales of a product or close a plant. Federal law only applies to products that cross state lines, products of about sixty thousand food processing and handling plants. As there are only two hundred federal food inspectors, the plants are inspected on the average of once every six years according to *The New York Times*. Although the effort is small, each year these inspections turn up hundreds of violations where food is unfit for consumption.

Many new standard foods are pre-prepared or precooked. Sometimes these foods are not cooked to a high enough temperature to kill bacteria. Final freezing of the product does not kill the bacteria either. Careless handling at home can result in the warm, wet conditions bacteria need. The FDA took samples from an ordinary chop suey mix one morning at a food plant. When removed from the refrigerator the mix contained six hundred bacteria per gram (safe). A few hours later the count was fifteen hundred, by early afternoon, 660,000. When ready for blast freezing in late afternoon, the count was up to ten million bacteria per gram. This batch was seized. To protect against contamination, food should be cooked at high temperatures and cooled to 40°or less within one or two hours. This is especially important for meat.

When buying meat, you should know the different grades. You should also know how the meat can be used and the amount of waste. Any federally graded meat is wholesome. The United States Department of Agriculture

Through its standards and guidelines for the food industry, the Food and Drug Administration provides protection for the consumer, who is guaranteed the right to have clean, healthful, truthfully labeled products.

grades beef and lamb (there are none for pork; chicken is graded A, B, or C.) The grades for beef and lamb are as follows: U.S.D.A. Prime—excellent flavor, marbling (even distribution of fat), lean; U.S.D.A. Choice—good quality, most popular grade; U.S.D.A. Good—little marbling, tougher cut, good for chopped meat or stews; U.S.D.A. Standard—little marbling and lacks juices; U.S.D.A. Commercial—the leanest, toughest, and least expensive. Not usually available, it is the only grade produced from mature animals.

These private grades that some supermarkets use, such as "A.O.K.," may vary as they wish. Check the government grade to be sure of reliability. But grade is not the only factor in buying meat. You should also look for the cut, or from what part of the animal the meat came. When buying beef the following is helpful:

1. Most tender: rib roasts, rib eye roasts, rib steaks, tenderloin, porterhouse, T-bone steaks, strip loin, club steaks, and sirloin steaks.
2. Moderately tender: rump roast, sirloin tip roast, blade chuck steak, round steaks.
3. Less tender: eye of round roasts, blade chuck roast, shoulder, arm chuck steak, flank steak.
4. Least tender: heel of round, shoulder arm roast, brisket.

These same general rules apply to pork and lamb as well. The least used muscles in the rib and loin areas are the tenderest. The shoulder (chuck) and the leg (ham) are always less tender but not necessarily less desirable.

Fish is not graded by the United States Department of Agriculture. When you buy fresh fish look for eyes that are bright and bulging, not glassy or sunken. The flesh should be firm, the gills red, and the odor pleasant. Fish is usually inexpensive when compared to beef, pork, or lamb. Comparisons should be made by the price per serving.

Shellfish should always be alive, frozen, or canned when bought.

Other foods may be discussed with the meat group because of their high protein content. Eggs as well as dried peas and beans are examples. Eggs are graded by the United States Department of Agriculture as AA (firm, thick), A (less firm), and B (general cooking). The highest grade (also called fresh fancy) is superior only because it has a better appearance when fried or poached. Buy Grade B for general cooking. C is a commercial grade. All grades are clean and wholesome. Shell color indicates no more than the breed of hen. Size refers to the weight of eggs per dozen: jumbo (30 oz. plus), extra large (27 oz.), large (24 oz.), medium (21 oz.), small (18 oz.), and pee wee (13 oz.). When large eggs sell for 60 cents a dozen, that's the same as 40 cents a pound for high protein food with large amounts of iron and vitamins A and B. Dry beans and peas are another economical way to serve needed protein in the diet. A pound of dried peas costing 20 cents can be used to prepare a 10 pound batch of thick soup at 2 cents a pound.

Milk and milk products are very popular. You can save money on your milk purchases by buying larger containers, cooking with dry or canned milk, and drinking skim milk. Pasteurized milk is germ free, clean, wholesome, and of uniform quality. Fresh milk must meet varying state standards. Vitamin D on a label means this rare sunshine vitamin needed for good health has been artificially added. Nonfat dry milk is made by removing the cream (and with it the milk's vitamins A and D) and the water. It is the least expensive milk product, stores easily, prevents waste, is high in protein and low in flavor because the milk sugar has been changed by harmless bacteria. Buttermilk and yogurt are examples. The food value of these is about the same as the milk from which they were made. Chocolate and flavored milk drinks are made from skim milk and are slightly watered down as well. Imitation milks must be clearly labeled. They are more economical but less nutritious than natural milk.

Other dairy products that count as milk servings are cheese and ice cream. Neither is covered by federal law. There are so many different ingredients in ice cream that it is difficult to assess the best buys. Generally speaking, ice cream must be differentiated from ice milk by a minimum quantity (usually 5%) of butter fat. Whatever tastes best at the lowest price is your best buy until labeling laws are passed regarding the nutritional content of ice cream.

Butter comes in three grades: AA, A, and B. The first two differ in flavor and texture, and the last is usually made from sour rather than from fresh cream. All U.S.D.A. grades are pure, clean, and wholesome. However, margarine, which is more economical than butter, is far better healthwise. Margarine contains vitamin A and low-cholesterol fats.

The fruit and vegetable group has a wide price range. Your best purchases are fresh fruit or vegetables in season, and frozen or canned the rest of the year. You should only buy fresh foods when you can use them in a short time. Do not buy damaged or over-ripe produce even if the price is low unless you intend to make jam or sauces immediately. Damage attracts the presence of bacteria, mold, or tiny insects. The best fresh fruit and vegetables are U.S.D.A. graded as No. 1 or fancy. These grades are used between farmers and buyers not between retail stores and the consumer. States and chain stores have their own grades as well. These sometimes have little real meaning for the consumer. You must learn to carefully judge the condition of each variety. Usually you look for high lustre, cleanliness, and firmness but not hardness. The pamphlets *How to Buy Fresh Vegetables* (U.S.D.A. H. and G. Bulletin 143) and *How to Buy Fresh Fruit* (U.S.D.A. H. and G. Bulletin 141) are available free from the United States Government Printing Office, Washington, D.C. 20402. The U.S.D.A. grades for canned and frozen vegetables and fruits in order of quality are: fancy (or A), extra standard (or B), and standard (or C). The differences are based on age, attractiveness, color blemishes, flavor, and tenderness. The fancy grade may be served hot or cold; grade B is good served hot or in gelatin salads, and grade C is satisfactory for soups, souffles, or purees. Another factor is the style. You pay more for whole vegetables, for those in special sauces or for fancy cuts. Dices, short cuts, and pieces are the least expensive. Nutritionally, there is a little difference between canned and frozen fruits and vegetables.

Breads and cereals have no federal quality standards. General labeling laws must be followed but otherwise differences must be determined by extensive and careful attention to the ingredients. House brand bakery products are usually the best buy. However, bakery goods are relatively expensive. Check the cost per pound and per serving. Compare to other available foods.

The pricing of food is often misleading. Especially confusing are strange price deals, for example, 7 for $1.57 or 1.6 lbs. for $1.43. Another misleading practice is selling products in odd shapes, odd measurements, or with cupped-in-bottoms. *The New York Times* has noted that a cereal selling at 37 cents for 4.75 ounces in a colorful larger-than-needed package was really $1.30 a pound—almost as much as a steak. Jennifer Cross, in her book *The Super Market Trap,* tells of the butcher who puts fancy names and prices on ordinary cuts of meat. For example, Manhattan steak is sold at $1.29 a pound instead of chuck steak at 89 cents

This pleasing display shows foods from three of the four basic groups. High protein fish and eggs offer a change of pace from meats, such as these thick chops. Also high in protein, milk and milk products are popular with all age groups. Delicious fresh vegetables are an excellent buy in season; they should be firm, lustrous, and undamaged.

a pound. Mrs. Cross also criticizes costly trading stamps, so-called premiums, and promotional games. She says the consumer pays one way or another. She also attacks "new improved" products that are neither new nor improved and colorful labels that misinform or mislead. She reports that you can save as much as 20% by doing the following:

1. Buy "house" brands—the products the store puts its name on.
2. Keep track of the prices of items you usually buy.
3. Watch advertisements for true specials. Compare stores and shop around.
4. Buy the largest sizes whenever reasonable.
5. Shop in supermarkets rather than small grocery stores unless looking for special items.
6. Shop at stores where *unit pricing* is easily understood. Tell the manager of stores which confuse pricing that more and more markets are clearly labeling the price per unit.

In New York City, Bess Meyerson,Grant, Commissioner of the Department of Consumer Affairs, tried to require some unit price labeling. This would list food products by the price per ounce or some other unit. Busy shoppers would then be able to compare the prices of competing products. Without unit pricing it would be difficult to determine whether 3 pounds for $1.77, 12 ounces for 47 cents, or 1 pound 1 ounce for 67 cents is the best buy. To get the correct answer, you must take the time to change each to ounces and divide the total ounces for each item by the price. This will give you the price per ounce. The correct item would not be chosen by most college educated housewives according to the January 1969 issue of *Consumer Reports*. There are simply too many different prices and package sizes for a busy shopper to do the arithmetic necessary to compare prices. In recent years, many supermarkets have introduced unit pricing. A growing number of states now have laws that require unit pricing in large stores.

The charge has often been made that unfair pricing is especially common in poverty areas. Among the complaints investigated were: 1) higher prices were charged in low income areas, and 2) poorer quality meat and produce were sold in low income areas. In 1969, a report to the Federal Trade Commission was made concerning food chain selling practices in Washington, D.C. and San Francisco. It was found that "area pricing" did exist and that it was based upon the threat of competition. Low-income neighborhoods are located in areas that are not growing. There is little competition. In the suburbs, however, rapid growth has brought new chain stores and strong competition. The investigation found that prices there are slightly lower. Poorer quality meat and produce were sold in lower income areas but generally at the usual low price. Here the stores appeared to meet the economic needs of their customers. The report stated that there was only a slight difference in pricing practices between high-and-low-income areas. Yet this fact is important. If possible, you should stop at stores where competition keeps prices lower and quality higher. These are more likely found in the fast growing areas.

Managing your food purchases involves the resources you have available: energy, time, money, skill in preparing food, and equipment for food storage. One resource may be used to make up for a weakness in another. For example, you may use time, skill, storage space, and energy to shop for low-priced tomatoes to make a 3-gallon batch of spaghetti sauce to be frozen. You'll save on a resource, money.

When making a shopping list, base it on your needs

and consider the following:

1. Out-of-season food costs more. Vegetables from greenhouses or from across the country are expensive. So check newspaper food ads for low prices of foods in season.
2. Keep a checklist handy to write down needs when supplies run low—then only buy what you have on the list. Avoid impulse buying.
3. Plan a menu for the week. Take into account the likes and dislikes of family members. Decide the quantity of each item needed.
4. Compare the costs of foods similar in food value. Although chicken is selling at one-third the cost of ham, the food value remains the same.
5. Match quality to use. Top grade vegetables are not necessary for soups or casseroles. A more flavorful rather than a more expensive, tender meat is needed for stews.
6. Compare costs per serving. One pound of bony spareribs may serve two in your family, but a pound of ground beef may serve four.
7. Watch the price of items as you select them and as they are rung up on the cash register. This week's "special" may have last week's price. Save your receipt to help establish your budget needs.
8. Make your own selection. Do not order by phone. Do not let the clerk choose your fresh foods unless you don't know how to find the best quality. If you don't know, learn.

Your efforts at economy are not ended with the best buy. Storage of food can be expensive and wasteful. Fresh meat and poultry should be wrapped loosely and placed in the coldest part of the refrigerator. The loose wrapping allows a little air in which causes slight drying on the surface of the meat. Smoked, cured, and cooked meats may be left in their original market paper. Fish should be wrapped tightly and used within a day or two. Before using, wash uncooked fish or seafood in cold running water. Eggs should be stored on their small ends. This keeps the yolk fresher. Food should be taken from the refrigerator only just before cooking or serving. Leftovers should be put in the refrigerator as soon as possible. Remember to use food in storage before eating freshly bought food.

You can get information about the selection, preparation, packaging, and storage of food from a wide variety of sources. Freezer manufacturers, such as Hotpoint Company, 5600 West Taylor Street, Chicago, Illinois, have free instructions and recipe booklets. Utility companies often have home service department booklets about stoves, refrigerators, freezers. So do county home economic extention services. Federal, state, or provincial Departments of Agriculture, Fisheries, and the Department of the Interior also have helpful materials. The United States Department of Agriculture, Washington, D.C. 20250, has an excellent recipe booklet *Freezing Combination Main Dishes* for 10 cents.

You can also save money when you cook. High protein foods, such as meat, eggs, or beans, should be cooked at moderate or low heat. High temperatures toughen protein and add to fuel costs. Use tested recipes and follow directions carefully when measuring. Use the recommended size and type of pans. Minor mistakes or changes can ruin an expensive meal. Correct methods of cooking will retain important nutrients, flavor, texture, and color. You save by avoiding waste and by getting your full food-value. For example, rice should never be washed before or after cooking. Important nutrients are lost. Casseroles or one-dish meals are inexpensive and nutritious. If you want more examples, the Superintendent of Documents, Government Printing Office, Washington, D.C. 20402, will send you a 10-cent booklet, *Conserving the Nutritive Value of Foods*. Other savings methods include the use of the leftover. Despite its poor reputation, the leftover can be tasty. Condiments, such as relishes, sauces, or mustard, can help. In the hands of a skilled cook, the humble leftover can be an economical and delicious meal.

CHAPTER REVIEW

I. GAINING KNOWLEDGE

Find the meaning of each of these words and phrases. Use each in a sentence of your own.

energy	protein
enriched	serving
marbling	vitamin
nutrition	

Match the following consumer goods with the standard used to grade them:

Product	Grade
1. pork loin roast	a. A
2. eggs	b. U.S.D.A. choice
3. rice	c. Fancy or A
4. canned beets	d. U.S.D.A. No. 1 or fancy
5. lamb chop	e. no grade
6. butter	f. AA
7. non-fat dry milk	g. U.S. extra

II. BUILDING SKILLS

Based on the information in the chapter, which of the following statements are true and which are false?

1. Amino acids are needed for a healthy diet.
2. Food additives are unsafe.
3. "Enriched" means that missing nutrients have been replaced.
4. Vitamin A is found in dark green or yellow vegetables.
5. The meat packing industry should lower its prices.
6. Most college-educated housewives are not able to shop economically without unit pricing.
7. Small neighborhood stores sell food at lower prices than prices offered in the chain stores.

III. EXPLORING VALUES

1. In 1798, Thomas Malthus wrote about the doom of mankind. He said the population would always multiply faster than the food supply. Is this true today?
2. The government should require all foods to have grade labels.
3. Chain stores which save the suburban shopper's money should be forced to open branches in ghetto areas and charge the same or lower prices.

IV. TAKING ACTION

1. Invite a home arts teacher in your school system to speak to the class concerning heavily advertised foods, such as candy bars, cold cereals, and snack desserts.
2. Write to your Congressman for information about a law or proposed law about packaging, labels, or grades of food. Ask him what his vote will be.
3. Invite a neighborhood store manager to the class to give inside tips on food buying and selling. Have him explain how prices are determined, the effect of displays upon the customers, and how foods are preserved. Ask him how a customer can get good service and the best food value.

CHAPTER THREE
FURNITURE AND APPLIANCES

Most Americans buy furniture twice in their lives: once when they are married, and the second time when their children have grown. Since each set has to last a generation or more, choices should be made with care. Develop a plan that fits your needs and your taste. Consider color, design, cost, storage capacity, durability, and use.

Purchase the items in order of priority: for example, don't buy a coffee table before you buy a kitchen table. Some items can be second-hand or unpainted. Look at your budget to figure out what you can afford to buy on your priority list. You may have to borrow money to purchase essential items; however, the non-essentials can wait.

Selecting furniture is difficult. Find a reputable dealer who has served friends or relatives well. So many different styles, woods, fabrics, stuffings, brands, and finishes are available, that you will need his professional knowledge. Tell him about your priority list, budget, and needs. If you live with a sharp clawed cat or a little brother, your furniture needs to be durable as well as beautiful. Ask the dealer about the necessary care required for each item and the quality of construction. Closely inspect each item yourself, and don't be afraid to turn chairs over or lift out upholstered sections. Check for:

1) Smooth, tight movement of doors and drawers.

2) Comfort of chairs and sofas.

3) Smooth rocking of rocking chairs.

4) Uniform smooth quality of finish. Use your fingernail on an unseen portion to test hardness.

5) Reinforcements at each point of stress such as corners.

6) Flat and firm stance on the floor.

7) Clean, even, dove-tailed joinings.

8) Hinges, zippers, and other rust-proof parts heavy enough to do their job for years.

9) Cheap materials used in unseen areas such as the back, inside and bottom.

Fabric and finish are also important. Check the government label to find the contents of the upholstery. Check the colors of the fabric and finish in the daylight, and ask about the possibility of fading and replacement of the fabric. Find out if the fabric is spot-proofed; since fabrics are graded by each manufacturer there is no uniform standard of quality. When looking at upholstered furniture, be sure that the area under the cushions is covered by the same fabric, and that all upholstery is firmly in place, especially where the fabric meets the wood. Look for heavy muslin coverings and strong covered coils. Read the required government labels on all stuffing and padding: avoid stuffings of shredded materials or non-tufted padding.

Be sure the wooden parts are hard woods. Select wood finishes that are scratch-resistant and waterproof. Lacquer finishes are better than varnish, and generally the more rugged a wood's appearance, the more abuse it can take. Solid wood is not necessarily the best, a coat of a superior wood that is glued to a sturdy base is generally superior in looks and durability. *Veneer* finishes can crack or chip if too thin; however, a final formica finish can resist chips, stains, acid, or burns.

After your selection is made, discuss the purchase

PHILIP TEUSCHER

This bedroom furniture is solid and durable as well as handsome. The room illustrates the beauty of simplicity and strict symmetry. Colorful bedspreads and drapes are tastefully coordinated.

with the dealer. In second-hand shops, bargaining over the price is common. Lower prices can usually be found during February and August. Only a few items, such as mattresses, carry guarantees and are usually *pro-rated.* This means the amount of money returned is determined by the extent of wear the item has received and the length of time it has been in a person's possession. Beware of quoted prices that do not include all the services: packing, delivery, and handling. If you are buying unpainted furniture, add the cost of finishing materials to the price to determine the true price to you. Your bill or contract should include dates of delivery, balance due, finance payments, and the model number of the specific purchased item. Do not pay the entire bill at the time of purchase. When your furniture arrives, inspect it while the delivery men are still there because complaints should be made immediately. Don't make the final payments until you are satisfied. If the dealer refuses to listen call the local Better Business Bureau.

Shopping for rugs and carpeting is similar to shopping for furniture. It is wise to go to several stores, and compare prices and quality. Be careful about warehouses or factory outlets; many of them have the same overhead costs and prices as regular stores. Buy padding for extra comfort and wear. When judging quality, look for the type and grade of the fiber and the construction of the yarn and the fabric. The construction is most important: depth and closeness of the *pile,* the weight of the yarn, and the strength of the backing all contribute to beauty and long wear. Generally speaking the deeper the pile, the better the rug. Read rug labels carefully; by law, each label should list:

1) The name of the maker or the Federal Trade Commission's number.
2) Country of origin.

3) Names of all fibers in the pile (the fibers in the backing are not required here).

4) The percentage of each fiber (for example, nylon, rayon, cotton, wool) if over 5 percent. (Only percentages over 20 have any effect upon the characteristics of the carpet.)

In one recent year, Americans bought 160 million appliances. There are hundreds of manufacturers and thousands of models. The consumer cannot know all he needs to know about each purchase, yet the Federated Department Stores chain found that most consumers did not read information when it was given. As an experiment, FDS attached labels with basic facts to 143 different appliances. After four months, a survey was taken. Less than half of the purchasers had not even noticed the tags; only one in five purchasers used the tags in making comparisons. Yet many appliances, such as refrigerators, last an average of fifteen years; such an investment should be made carefully. Others, such as built-in microwave ranges or vacuum systems, may cost over $1500, a considerable dent in the family budget. Careless purchase may stay with a family and the family budget for a long time.

When buying appliances, there are a number of tips to keep in mind. Because many appliances are primarily convenience items, their purchase should be weighed against their cost: be certain they meet your needs and purposes, determine the proper size and capacity, and be sure you have the space and electrical facilities to make them work. The wiring load, outlet locations, and cables in your home should be checked to service large appliances. Most cities and towns have safety regulations concerning wiring and installations. Remember to consider the cost of installation, plumbing, or rewiring when making purchases. You will pay an extra 20 percent over the purchase price

QUALITY STANDARDS FOR APPLIANCES

TYPE OF APPLIANCES	GRADE MARK	MEANING
Electrical equipment	U.L.	Equipment has been tested by Underwriters Laboratories. (Label on cord may only apply to the cord itself.)
Air conditioners	NEMA seal	The claimed BTU (British thermal unit) cooling capacity has complied with Electrical Manufacturers Association.
Gas ranges	Blue Star Gold Star	The American Gas Association basic standards are met for sturdiness, safety, and cooking performance. Gold star indicates deluxe models.
Refrigerators	NEMA certification	Claimed net volume and shelf area meet NEMA standards.
Water heaters	NEMA or AGA seal	Claimed recovery rate and other features meet NEMA or AGA standards.

QUALITY STANDARDS FOR BEDDING

The National Association of Bedding Manufacturers recommends that an adult have a sleeping space 38 inches wide and about 6 inches longer than his height. The mattress should be firm enough to keep a spine on a straight line. Matresses come in these standard sizes:

single youth	30x75 inches	king size	76x80 inches
twin	38x75 inches	twin extra long	38x80 inches
double regular	53x75 inches	full extra long	53x80 inches
queen size	60x80 inches		

to service the appliance over its average life. Choose the dealer carefully: be sure repair services are readily available. Second-hand items of high quality can be a better value than new, low quality goods. The brand names are a safer buy because parts are easy to get and service men are well trained. Brand name products usually carry better *warranties* which need to be read carefully. They are designed to protect the manufacturer rather than the consumer. Courts have ruled that the manufacturer is responsible for any damage caused by defective parts. In response, manufacturers have put a time limit upon this responsibility. The average warranty runs for ninety days. A *guarantee,* protecting the consumer, is usually offered by retail stores for brand names only. These guarantees can be misleading; be sure they cover the entire unit, not just the more durable parts. To protect yourself further, look for the product ratings of the various brands in *Consumer Reports* and *Consumer Bulletin.*

When you examine the appliance itself, check its features carefully. Of primary importance is safety. Ask yourself if small children could easily hurt themselves on any of the fixtures. The amount of current necessary to light a 15-watt bulb can kill you. Are switches and wiring well protected? Do you have a three-prong plug for grounding to prevent shocks? Can the item be cleaned, stored, moved, and serviced easily? Are doors, handles, lights, insulation, outer and inner finishings all well constructed? Are serial numbers attached and controls easy to read? Note the electrical current required, and compare the horsepower or wattage available to other items. Current is measured in amperes (amps): a one hundred watt lamp bulb uses one amp and a 250-watt iron uses twelve. Your electrical system must be able to carry the amp load you require; if it does not, fire may result from wires overheating.

Read the instruction manual. Can you operate the appliance? Try it *yourself.* When you buy, be sure the salesman writes any promises or unwritten guarantees on the sales slip. Keep the sales slip and all tags that can help you exchange, clean, or replace parts.

Unquestionably you will have some problems with appliances, but some of them can be avoided or repaired without the help of a serviceman. The head of a repair company states that almost half his calls could be avoided if people looked at the appliance manual to see if they had been exercising proper care. First check the following: fuses, plugs, safety start switches, venting, and controls. Make certain the appliance is clean and not overloaded. Inspect the wiring for frays and damage. If you cannot solve the problem, contact the *warrantor,* or person who issued the warranty, immediately. Delay may cause the warranty to expire.

Do not try major repairs yourself unless you are experienced. Your repairman may be unable to undo the damage you may cause. All service calls are expensive. The more time it takes to do the job, the more it costs you. If the serviceman, retailer, or manufacturer refuses to give proper service, you should write to the Major Appliance Consumer Action Panel at 20 North Wacker Drive, Chicago, Illinois 60606. The local Better Business Bureau can also help. If all else fails, it is the job of the state consumer commissioner in your state capital to help.

CHAPTER REVIEW

I. GAINING KNOWLEDGE

Find the meaning of each of these words and phrases. Use each in a sentence of your own.

electric grounding	overhead
fabric, yarn, pile	pro-rated
guarantee	warranty

II. BUILDING SKILLS

Choose the correct answer.

1. Which of the following must be labeled according to federal law? a) springs, b) fabric, c) wood, d) stuffing.
2. Electrical current is measured in amperes. Which of the following circuits overloads a 15-amp circuit? a) 2 lamps and an iron, b) 12 lamps, c) 2 irons, d) iron and a lamp.
3. According to an established appliance dealer, nearly half of his regular calls are caused by a) faulty wiring, b) not reading instructions, c) crime, d) people who want to play cards.
4. According to a chain department store survey, only a few shoppers read information tags. The number who do is a) 1 in 3, b) 1 in 4, c) 1 in 5, d) 1 in 10.
5. The Federal Government requires all of the following on a rug label except: a) fibers in pile, b) name of manufacturer, c) country of origin, d) fibers in backing.

III. EXPLORING VALUES

Do you agree or disagree with the following? Why?

1. A home should have beautiful furniture or a comfortable lived-in look.
2. If you buy a mattress falsely labeled *all-horse hair* and *Made in U.S.A.* and discover it is really made of inferior materials, what would you do? If the dealer tried to keep you from talking by giving you all your money back, and put the mislabeled mattress back on sale, what action would you take?

IV. TAKING ACTION

1. Set up a list of the hidden costs of owning appliances. First list all common appliances and their price. Then note maintenance, operating, and installment costs. Compare these costs to the purchase price. Which items now appear to be the bargains?

2. Make a survey of appliance owners among friends and relatives to discover how safe their electrical appliances are (U.L. approval). Carefully prepare questions that survey how knowledgeable they are concerning safe operation. You might ask "what is the wiring load allowed in your home?" Report the results of your survey to the class. Then bring safety information back to the appliance owners.

3. Invite a qualified electrician to speak to the class concerning proper installation and proper wiring.

4. Write for one of the following consumer information guides.

Carpets and Rugs, The Now Way to Choose Them, 25 cents. *Carpet and Rug Care Guide,* Department of Public Relations, Carpet and Rug Institute, Box 2048, Dalton, Georgia 30720. Send stamped, self-addressed envelope.

How to Select Floor Coverings, How to Select Major Home Appliances, How to Select Window Treatments, Let's Decorate the Bathroom, How to Select Paint and Wall Covering for Your Home, 10 cents each from: C.I.S. Department 704, Public Relations, Sears Roebuck and Co., 7401 Skokie Boulevard, Skokie, Illinois 60076.

Testing at Consumer's Research, $5 rental, *Safety in the Home,* $5 rental, Color Slide Sets, Consumer's Research, Inc., Washington, N.J. 07882.

Your Equipment Dollar, 25 cents from: N.F.C., Prudential Plaza, Chicago, Illinois 60601.

CHAPTER FOUR
CARE AND USE OF CLOTHING

Several considerations contribute to your choice of a wardrobe: your size, your budget, your taste, and your profession. Certain principles will help you in making wise decisions:

1) List your needs in order of priority.
2) Choose basic styles to dress up or down for different occasions. For example, a high quality sweater may be worn to school or to informal parties.
3) Plan around one group of colors so that all your clothes go well together. Then you can mix and match more items.
4) Look for multi-season clothes that can be used with various accessories at different times of the year.
5) Select shoes and other accessories, such as ties, scarves, and gloves, that will blend well.
6) Avoid extremes in color style and fashion; they are difficult to match.

In order to keep a budget, compare values. The middle prices are often more economical in the long run than high or low priced items. Low priced items are usually unsatisfactory; high priced items do not necessarily give the extra wear for the extra money. Look for sales, especially seasonal sales; for example, a winter coat bought at a January sale is often half price. Select only those items on your list that have a specific purpose in your wardrobe. Be sure to try on most clothing, because reliable standards for sizes still do not exist. Garments, such as men's shirts, are an exception to this rule. Learn all you can about quality workmanship which includes such features as the following:

1) Reinforcement at points of strain, such as pockets, knees, and elbows.
2) Buttons and buttonholes well matched and placed, firmly stitched, and bound.
3) Stitching that is straight, neat, secure, close, and properly colored.
4) Seams and hems which are even, flat, and secure with allowances for adjustments.
5) Generous cut and fabric allowances. Fabric that is cut with the grain, not on the cross grain.
6) Designs matched at the seams.
7) Zippers well placed, covered, and securely attached.
8) Linings and padding properly placed and of proper material.

Gaining knowledge about fabrics is essential in order to shop well. You should learn to gauge how much the item will cost not only initially, but also in the long run. Dry cleaning bills add considerably to the initial cost of the item, and some fabrics simply last longer than others. Check labels that list fiber content and cleaning instructions. The 1960 Federal Textile Fiber Products Identification Act, enforced by the Federal Trade Commission, requires that the more than seven hundred trade names of artificial fibers be classified within one of seventeen named groups. Once you learn the seventeen groups you don't need to know the seven hundred. Six are well known: rubber, glass, metallic, rayon, nylon, and acetate. Four others are commonly known: acrylic, saran, polyester, and vinyl. The remaining are not well known: modacrylic, azlon, spandex, olefin, nytril, vinyon, and anidex.

Natural fiber must also be named as a percentage of a garment's fiber content. When you buy you should keep the tag or label for washing or dry cleaning reference. Special treatments include such characteristics as colorfast, spot repellant, wrinkle-resistant, drip-dry, wash and wear, permanent press (these last four are in order of their ironing needs), and preshrunk. This last characteristic is important for wool or cotton. If these natural fibers can shrink more, the percentage of possible shrinkage must be listed on the label. Natural fibers are made by plants (linen, cotton) or animals (silk, wool). The Wool Labeling Act of 1940 requires that all wool products be clearly labeled. Camels, sheep, goats, lamb, llamas, alpaca, and vicuna all produce the fleece legally called wool. The percentage of the kinds of wool in a fabric must also be given on the label.

According to Mr. C.F. Meyers, chairman of Burlington Industries, there has been a dramatic and continuing shift from natural fibers to the use of man-made or chemically manufactured fibers. In an article in *The New York Times,* Mr. Meyers stated that the entire textile industry is investing in the future of these fibers and research has already developed dozens of fibers with widely differing characteristics. For example, saran is expansive, tough, and durable. It resists water, sunlight, abrasions, stains, chemicals, insects, wrinkles, and fire. It is excellent for use in luggage, auto seat covers, doll's hair, draperies, upholstery, and carpeting.

Fabric construction refers to fibers or yarns (fibers twisted together) that are knitted, woven or matted. Matted fabrics are non-woven fibers and generally not very durable. Felt and muslin are examples. Woven fabrics generally keep their shape better because the yarns are interlaced at right angles to each other. Knitted fabrics consist of yarns that

	NATURAL FIBERS				MAN-MADE FIBERS							
Characteristics	Cotton	Linen	Silk	Wool	Acetate	Triacetate	Rayon	Spandex△	Acrylic	Nylon	Polyester	Olefin
Natural resistance to:												
Abrasion	*			*					*	*	*	*
Wrinkling			*	*	*	*			*	*	*	*
Shrinkage									*	*	*	*
Waterborne stains									*	*	*	*
Sunlight				*	*	*			*		*	
Perspiration								*				
Mildew					*				*	*	*	*
Moths		*			*	*	*	*	*	*	*	*
Flammability			*	*					*	*	*	
Resilience			*	*	*			*	*	*	*	*
Shape retention			*				*	*	*	*	*	
Versatility	*			*			*				*	*
Durability	*	*		*				*	*	*	*	*
Strength	*	*	*				*	*	*	*	*	*
Absorbency	*	*	*	*	*		*					
Quick drying		*			*			*	*	*	*	*
Subject to fume fading					*	*						
Heat sensitive			*		*			*	*	*	*	*
Care:												
Dry cleaning preferred			*	*			*					
Hand or machine washable	*	*		†	*	*			*	*	*	*
Avoid Chlorine bleach††			*	*	*			*				
Avoid strong detergents		*	*	*				*				
Wash whites separately									*	*	*	*
Dry shortest and lowest cycle									*	*	*	*
Iron damp, wrong side, low heat			*		*	*				*	*	*
Iron damp, wrong side, moderate to hot heat	*	*					*					
Needs little ironing				*					*	*	*	*
Pretreat oil-borne stains									*	*	*	*

△   Spandex is only used in combination with other fibers to produce stretch fabrics

†† Avoid chlorine bleach for any fabrics with drip-dry finish

†   Some woolens are machine washable

are looped together. These include traditional sweaters as well as the newer double knits. According to the consumer magazine, *Changing Times,* double knitted fabrics are now as popular as woven fabrics. Double knits are more elastic, cool, wrinkle-free, and comfortable than the traditional stiff woven fabrics. You can move more easily in a tight knit than a woven fabric, but it costs more and snags easily.

Quality is all important in the buying of clothing accessories and footwear. Your shoes directly affect your comfort and health. Never wear a shoe that does not fit well; avoid letting your younger brothers or sisters wear your out-grown shoes. A child's bones are soft and pliable, and permanent damage may result. To get the best possible fit, ask the salesman to measure both feet each time you buy; try both shoes on with the hosiery you will wear with them since the thickness may make a difference; and stand with your weight on both feet to check their comfort. In open shoes or sandals, neither toe nor heel should be over the edge of the sole. The widest part of the shoe should fit the widest part of your foot.

Accessories, such as scarves, ties, belts, gloves, hats, handbags, and jewelry, can be expensive and should be chosen carefully. Jewelry should fit in with your outfit. Expensive gold or silver jewelry should be bought from jewelers you can trust. Costume jewelry is more adaptable to rapid changes in the fashion world and you don't need to spend much money on it. The International Ladies Garment Workers Union, a division of A.F.L./C.I.O. offers seven free booklets with information on fashion for women and girls. To obtain them, write Consumer Service Division, I.L.G.W.U., 275 7th Avenue, New York, New York 10001. Once clothing purchases are made, it is important to give them proper care. Many fabrics can be machine laundered;

some must be dry cleaned. You can help the professional cleaner by knowing:

1) the cause of stains
2) the fibers, fabric, and any special instructions on the original label
3) where to identify small holes and tears that may become enlarged in the cleaning process

You should tell the cleaner what measures you have used to try to remove the stain. Give him the measurements of knitted garments so that they may be blocked to size. Your best protection is to prevent any fabric from becoming over-soiled, which damages fabrics. You can help your budget by using economical coin-operated dry cleaning machines yourself for routine jobs. Shake and hang clothes immediately after cleaning to air them thoroughly.

Proper storage of your seasonal clothes adds to their life. Wash them without adding starch or dry clean them before storing. Ironing is not necessary. If you have enough space, store your clothes in a closet that is continually in use. Select a cool dry place to prevent mildew; hang clothes on wooden or padded hangers in garment bags; store sweaters and knit garments flat. Use mothproofing agents to protect clothing, especially woolens. Lastly, label your containers.

CHAPTER REVIEW

I. GAINING KNOWLEDGE

Find the meaning of each of these words and phrases. Use each in a sentence of your own.

accessories

content

cross grain

fleece

fiber

natural fiber

preshrunk

II. BUILDING SKILLS

Time yourself to see how long it takes you to answer the following three questions. You should be able to find the information and write it down in seven minutes. If you can do this in less than seven minutes, you have good skill in skimming for information. If it takes you longer, practice will improve your skill.

1) Which clothing usually gives you the best value in the long run; low priced, middle priced, or high priced?
2) When examining clothing for workmanship, what should you expect of a good lining?
3) How many fiber groups are legally recognized by the 1960 Textile Fiber Products Identification Act?

III. EXPLORING VALUES

Do you agree or disagree with the following? Why?

1. A family should expect teen-agers to pay for their own clothes.
2. New fashions each year are a must for good grooming.

IV. TAKING ACTION

Do one or more of the following.

1. Write to the National Retail Trade Merchants Association, 100 West 31st Street, New York, New York 10001, for a copy of the *Guide for Permanent Care Labeling* which explains latest F.T.C. label regulations.

2. Obtain *Stain Removal* (free) from the Association of Home Appliance Manufacturers, 20 North Wacker Drive, Chicago, Illinois 60606. Set up class demonstrations to show how each of thirty-two different stains can be removed.

3. Invite a dry cleaning expert to speak to the class concerning the proper home care and storage of your clothes.

4. Obtain samples of all seventeen types of fabrics and demonstrate to the class the properties of each.

5. Write to the Superintendent of Documents, Washington, D.C. for the thirty-page booklet, *Clothing Repairs*. Enclose 25 cents.

CHAPTER FIVE
PLANNING AN INSURANCE PROGRAM

The cost of medical care has become so great that the expense for a common operation can deplete a family's savings. Two weeks off your job and in the hospital can be a financial disaster. The average daily cost of a hospital room is over $80 a day, and this figure does not include doctor's fees or medication. According to the Health Insurance Institute's *Source Book,* medical costs have gone up faster in recent years than any other major item of personal expense. Americans now spend 7 percent of their budgets on medical needs, and costs continue to rise due to two causes: shortage of doctors and other medical people; and the poor distribution of manpower and health care facilities. The best way to meet your finanical risk in view of this national problem is health insurance. Various programs can help in six basic ways:

1) Regular medical insurance may cover doctor's house calls, office visits, all accident costs, testing services such as X-rays, the costs of an illness lasting a week to a month. This is basic protection only.

2) Major Medical Insurance covers long term disability whether caused by accident or illness.

3) Hospital expense insurance usually provides two benefits: one for daily room and board and one for additional hospital expenses such as anesthesia, drugs, use

of the ambulance, or use of the operating room.

4) Surgical expense benefits usually list all operations which are covered. Surgery for birth control purposes or plastic surgery for improving one's looks are not included.

5) Disability income insurance provides an income while you are unable to work.

6) Workman's Compensation laws are state insurance programs that cover some medical costs and loss of earning power. In most states you can receive weekly cash payments of $100 or two-thirds of your wages, whichever is lower.

When you buy health insurance remember to check:

1) the *option of insurability* which means you can increase benefits and premiums later without taking a new medical exam.

2) *the grace period* which keeps a policy in force (usually thirty-one days) after the premium was due but not paid.

3) your existing protection—you may already be covered to some extent by union benefits, parts of your life insurance, government programs, or a fraternal organization. Some policies will not pay if you have collected from another company.

4) how benefits compare to the actual local costs. The costs in different areas vary widely.

5) all coverage that you need must be in writing. Remember no policy covers anything not specifically stated in writing.

6) the ways that partial and total disability are defined. The policy may only accept the loss of both arms and legs as *disability*, for example.

7) when your present coverage expires. Newlyweds or students reaching their twentieth birthday have dis-

covered at a bad moment that dad's policy no longer applies. College policies, union policies, armed service policies, and employee policies end when your membership ends.

8) the risks which you are most likely to face, those which create large losses and costs if the worst happens.

Group health insurance programs became popular during World War II when wages were *frozen*. Companies tried to attract workers to their plants by offering *fringe benefits*. After the war, continued prosperity and union activity brought over 80 percent of American workers the benefits of group insurance. The employer usually paid all or most of the *premium*. Workers sometimes shared in the cost, then the costs were deducted from their paychecks by the employer and sent to the insurance company. Most of the health insurance now owned is group rather than private, Blue Cross and Blue Shield being among the most common group plans, although the Kaiser plan is gaining in popularity as well. In the Kaiser plan the group owns its own medical facilities.

Group plans are becoming popular in all insurance fields: life, medical, income, disability, and property. Under the laws of most states, group insurance may be sold wherever a group of five or more persons with a common purpose may be found. The larger the group, the lower the cost. Most group programs have age steps on which the *premiums* are based. This is your cost to purchase the insurance. The premium is higher as you get older or the *benefits* get lower as you get older. The insurance is always for a limited period of time and called *term* insurance. It is renewable on a yearly basis. Although companies can drop a policy at the end of the term, they almost never do. The business from the group as a whole is important to the insurance company. No one individual is left without protection when he needs it most. A second advantage is that rates are much lower than private rates. A third advantage is that group policies are written by well-established companies or organizations that are reliable and safe.

Unemployment insurance protects three of every four American workers. All employers must pay a special tax into a federal and state government fund. This fund pays as much as $55 a week for up to thirty-nine weeks for each time a former employee is unable to hold or find a job. This period may be extended by the Federal Government for areas having special employment problems. No private insurance companies can provide such protection; to collect you must fill out forms at your state employment office located in most larger cities.

Property insurance should protect you from possible losses. Because hazards vary with local conditions, no complete list of property insurance coverage is given. If you face unusual risks, you should have special insurance that covers them. Among the types of property insurance available are: fire insurance, theft insurance, baggage insurance, and liability insurance.

There are so many dangers for which you can be held responsible that it is wise to protect yourself against being sued. This happens when a person brings you to court. He would ask the court to have you pay for the damage or harm he suffered because of something you did. A court ruling could cost you a great amount of money. To guard against this, insurance companies sell *liability* insurance. Liability insurance may protect you:

   1) if someone injures himself on your property;

   2) if you incur damage on the property of another;

   3) if your dog or other pet inflicts injury on a human being.

A personal liability policy that covers you for losses of $25,000 will usually cover the claims previously mentioned and many others as well. A large lawsuit could cause you to lose your savings, your property, and even leave you with a continuing claim against all your future income. Liability insurance is not expensive, and it provides for broad coverage for all members of your family including your pets.

Most people save money by purchasing a standard homeowner's *package* policy which protects them from a number of common hazards. They commonly save 10 to 20 percent over the cost of buying single-purpose policies, and they have only one policy with one payment to worry about. Three common policies are listed on page 58. Homeowner's policies usually provide a sum to pay the expenses of living elsewhere if your home is destroyed, medical costs up to $500 for minor home accidents, even provides for the cost of bail bonds up to $500. The comprehensive policy is often called an *all-risks* policy, but it is not. Read the fine print in the policy.

If you buy property insurance you should follow the path that others have found best. Study carefully the risks to which you are exposed, and try to end some risks by changing conditions which might cause a loss. Transfer the remaining chance of loss to an insurance company. Make an inventory of everything you own, write down the cost of each item and the date it was bought. Keep this list with your other insurance policies in a safe deposit box in a bank. In the event of fire, you will still have a record of what each item is worth. Rare items of unusual worth should be appraised to find their true dollar value. This will insure prompt payment.

First establish the value of replacing your home. Call a reliable company that is approved by your state insurance

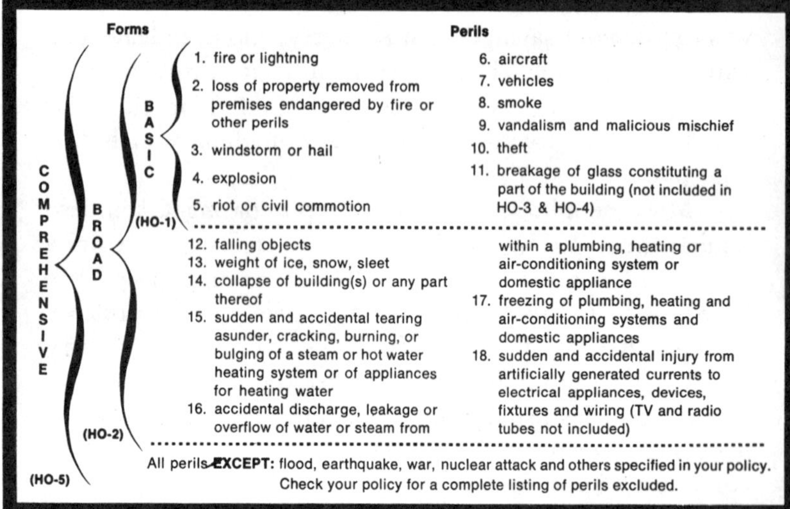

commissioner. What policies does the company offer to you? Some policies provide coverage for 80 percent of the value of your property, others may offer 100 percent coverage of the market value. Some will include safeguards against inflation. Your coverage goes up automatically as the premium goes up too. If you do not have this *inflation clause,* review your needs every three or four years. Read the policy with all attached *riders* carefully before signing; make sure that you know the meaning of all terms. Be sure that you know the cost of your policy, and the time it is in force. You should also know exactly what is covered and what exceptions are stated in the policy. In the event that you have to use the policy you should know how to report your losses.

Call several companies to compare costs and coverage: premiums for the same basic protection vary greatly. Once you have narrowed the field, meet with the agents. Buy only from an agent who deals with you in a way you completely understand.

If your property is damaged get your claim in promptly with a sworn statement. Then you should see if you need to buy more insurance. As a rule, the loss is deducted from the face value of the policy, and you will have less protection than before. Remember the company will only pay actual market value at the time of loss. Your 1961 oil painting by Jackson Pollack is worth more with passing time; your 1972 car is worth less.

Everyone likes to be master of his own fate. We Americans value independence. Yet sometimes fate can strike down the strongest among us. If at this very moment you were to be disabled by a terrible accident, what would be your fate? If you could not work, who would care for you? Who would care for your aging parents? From what source would come clothing, shelter, and medicine? If there is no certain answer, is this independence?

Such questions have always bothered Americans. The answer in colonial times was the family and the life-long friends in the town church, but as cities grew and people moved, life-long friends became few and the family became smaller. New answers were found. Public charity totally supported eighty-eight people in Boston in 1736; hundreds of widows received public assistance, yet pride rebelled against the possibility of public charity. Benjamin Franklin at the age of sixteen was one of the first to suggest the idea of life insurance and called it "the cheapest and safest mode of making a certain provision for one's family." The idea was to transfer the risk of disaster from one person and his family to a company. The few victims of disaster would be supported by the many who contributed a fee or premium for this purpose.

One cause for the need of protection is an early death. A "life" insurance policy provides for payment to the beneficiary (usually the wife and children) upon the death of the person upon whom they are dependent for their livelihood. Such people might be a wife and young children, aged parents, an invalid brother, or any dependent person.

Since 1934, some protection has been provided by Social Security. The Social Security program is intended to give workers and their families a basic floor of protection. After retirement and in case of death or disability, payments related to previous earnings are made. The program is organized by the Federal Government and supported by a small tax on both employee and employer. You now pay 5.85 percent on the first $10,800 of your earnings and will qualify for benefits after forty quarter-year employment periods in which you earned more than $50 and in which you paid the Social Security tax. As Social Security only provides a poverty-level standard of living, you need more insurance even after you qualify for benefits. Some occupations are not included in the Social Security program. Federal Government employees, teachers, doctors, members of charitable organizations, and farmers must look to their own insurance plans for security.

Social Security benefits include a small burial sum and monthly payments. A widow receives payments both for child-rearing and for retirement. When the youngest child reaches eighteen, the child rearing benefits stop; the retirement income starts when the widow reaches sixty or sixty-two. A wife may also receive a monthly disability benefit if her husband is totally disabled. According to the *Life Insurance Fact Book*, the average monthly payment is still well under $100, although this amount is being steadily increased, and it is an important part of insurance planning.

Still most families do not have adequate insurance coverage. Of course a single person with no dependents needs no insurance if his savings will pay his debts and burial costs; nor does a newly married couple need insurance if both are working. However, the arrival of a child alters the picture. Now the father will wish to provide for his children and for his widow who will need to care for them. Social Security payments will help, but they are not enough.

At this point the family usually consults an insurance agent. The agent should advise the family in their interests, but, being human, he generally thinks of his own interests first. Unfortunately his interests and theirs are not the same. It is for this reason that Consumers Union has issued the booklet entitled *The Consumers Union Report on Life Insurance.* The editors of *Consumer Reports* prepared this booklet for consumers. It should be read by everyone before purchasing life insurance. The first-year commission is by far the largest the life insurance agent will receive, hence he will generally try to sell you the policy that requires a large premium payment the first year. But this may not be the policy that offers you the protection you need.

The two major types of protection are *term insurance* and *cash value insurance.* It is important to understand the difference. Term insurance is life insurance and nothing else. Cash value insurance is life insurance plus savings. It may also be called straight, standard, or ordinary life insurance. For example, at age twenty-five, a husband wishing $50 thousand life insurance for his family might purchase ordinary life insurance by paying an annual premium of $632.50. Or he might purchase term insurance (five-year renewable) by paying the annual premium of $195.30. The reason for the difference is that the company is building up a savings account for the ordinary policy. This policy has a cash value which he can claim at any time. The longer he is insured the greater the cash value. This cash-value policy may be used as security to get low cost savings or cash value. At age thirty-five the cost of the policies would be $909.50 a year for straight life and $258.60 a year for the first five years of a five-year renewable term.

Five-year renewable term means that at the end of the first five years the policy may be renewed for five more years at a higher annual premium payment. When purchasing term insurance be sure that the policy is guaranteed renewable. Otherwise the company may require you to take a physical examination at the end of any five-year term. If your physical condition declines, you may be denied insurance when you need it most. The policy should be renewable at least until age sixty or even beyond if the insurance premiums are steep, but most heads of families will have fewer responsibilities by that time and will be able to reduce coverage.

If you buy term insurance you will pay much less than you would for straight life insurance. Suppose you invest the difference at a 6 percent return or better. Between the age of twenty-five and sixty-five you would build a cash reserve that would be worth about twice the cash value of a straight life policy. Even more important, if the insured dies, his estate includes the face value of his insurance policy *plus* this cash. But if he has straight life insurance, his estate from the policy is never worth more than the face value. If he uses the difference in insurance premium payments to help pay a mortgage on a house, he will be building a very valuable asset. With inflation the resale value of the house will increase. If instead he buys straight life insurance, the company must pay him about 3½ percent interest on his money. When he surrenders the policy the cash value would be less than the value of any reasonable investment he might have made.

In short, most agents who sell straight life insurance are not fully protecting the buyer. To get the most for your insurance money you should consult an impartial insurance counselor. Guaranteed renewable term insurance is likely to be your best buy. Good sources of insurance are savings banks, insurance on your job (where part or all of the premium is paid by your employer), veteran's insurance (for World War II and Korea but not Viet Nam). A company run for special groups, such as Teachers Insurance and Annuity Association of America, may also offer good life insurance.

In paying premiums you save money by annual rather than semi-annual or quarterly payments. Beware of industrial options; their premiums are very high. Always ask for a sample policy before purchasing. Read it carefully. See what it says about suicide, accidental death, waiver of premium in case of disability, and guarantee of renewability. Who has the right to renew the policy, you or the company? Be sure you do. Avoid buying by mail; your agent may be too far away. Beware of the twister, the salesman who tries to convince you to drop your old policy for his better policy. Usually the older the policy, the better for you. Consult both companies, get the new benefits in writing, and make your own decision. Remember that the purpose of insurance is protection of dependents. The breadwinner should be insured to at least five times his annual income.

Social Security, real estate, stocks and bonds, and

savings and annuities are all protection devices. Review your needs every few years. Most families become under-insured. Locate a safe place for your policy. Be sure you have a copy of the number of the policy and the address of the company and agent in another location. Other people concerned should be informed of both locations and the benefits involved.

In order to figure out your family needs, put yourself in the position of the administrator of your family's estate. You will find that most family needs can be divided into five main areas. These will describe the total dollar needs that your family will have from the date of your father's death well into the future. The second part will show the income that you now have that will offset the needs shown in part 1. Any difference will be what you need in order for your family to be totally secure.

1) Estimate immediate cash to cover final expenses. Include unpaid bills, medical expenses, unpaid notes, taxes, (property, state, federal, estate, and inheritance). Also include six months living income for your family based upon current salary ________________ $ ____

2) Amount needed to pay off mortgage (use the present unpaid value) ____________________ $ ____

3) Educational needs of children not yet through school. While costs will vary, allow a minimum of $2,000 per year per child for each year of training beyond high school $— x number of children x 4 = ______ $ ____

4) Annual living expense during the time that children are under age eighteen and mother is not yet age sixty-two. $— x number of years until youngest is age eighteen = ____________________ $ ____

5) Annual living expense for mother after children are age eighteen. $ x number of years to age eighty= ____________________ $ ____

Total Dollars Needed _________________________________$ _____

The needs listed above are offset by the following assets that can or will produce income on a when necessary basis. Disregard for this purpose all assets that are non-income producing or those that are not negotiable.

1) Social Security (per annum) while children are still minors ___________________________________$ _____

2) Face value of life insurance (in thousands)
   permanent ______________________________________$_____
   term or group_____________________________________ $ _____

3) Cash value of pension plan_______________________ $_____

4) Savings _______________________________________ $ _____

5) Income producing property (stocks, bonds, investments) _______________________________________ $_____

Total Monies Available____________________________ $_____

The difference between A and B (the amount needed in life insurance policies)_______________________ $_____

Chances are this figure is higher than you expected. A lot more dollar protection may be needed right now. Dollars needed to:

1) cover immediate expenses for the first six months
2) pay off remaining mortgage
3) pay for the desired education of children
4) cover living expenses of each child to independence
5) cover living expenses of mother, first to age sixty-two and then living expenses minus Social Security benefits to age eighty (average lifespan)

_________Total (A)

Dollars available when needed:

1) social security benefits
2) face value of life insurance
3) cash value of pension plan
4) savings
5) income producing property, such as stocks, bonds, in-

vestments

__________Total (B)

Differences between A and B (equals amount needed in life insurance.)

__________Total (C)

CHAPTER REVIEW

I. GAINING KNOWLEDGE

Find the meaning of each of these words and phrases. Use each in a sentence of your own.

benefit	grace period
coverage	liability
deductible	premium
dependent	riders
equity	term
estate	waiver

II. BUILDING SKILLS

Choose the phrases that best complete the statement.

1. If you lose your home in a fire, your homeowner's policy will usually pay you:
   the value of the land and home
   the market value of the home
   the face value of the policy
   the original price of the home
2. If you do not own your own home but want to insure your coin collection from theft, you should buy insurance that is:
   basic
   broad

    comprehensive

    exceptional

3. High medical costs are caused by all of the following except:

    shortage of doctors

    duplicate health care facilities

    poor distribution of manpower

    shortage of insurance programs

4. Life insurance premiums cost the most when they are paid:

    annually

    semi-annually

    quarterly

    monthly

5. Insurance companies make loans against life insurance policies and charge:

    no interest

    high interest

    low interest

    compound interest

6. You may qualify for Social Security after you have worker for:

    forty years

    money

    forty quarter-years in which you earned more than $50 per quarter

III. EXPLORING VALUES

1. Social Security provides minimum security for some Americans. Most of them have no choice as to whether they should belong to the program or not. Explore the attitudes of the following people regarding each question:

a) For teachers and senior citizens—should all Americans be made to join the Social Security program?

b) For senior citizens and young workers—should the

benefits (and taxes) be increased?

c) For students and middle aged parents—should coverage begin at ten instead of forty quarters?

d) For insurance agents, low income and high income people—does the program provide security?

IV. TAKING ACTION

1. Obtain an insurance policy, study it carefully, and explain it to other members of the class. Point out the legal terms, the strengths and weaknesses of the contract.

2. Invite a member of the local Better Business Bureau or an insurance counselor to class to discuss proper and improper selling practices currently used in the insurance market.

3. All state governments have departments responsible for overseeing the insurance industry. Write to one asking for a speaker to explain the department's interpretation of a policyholder's rights. How does his department help the consumer? Ask him to provide examples.

CHAPTER SIX
PURCHASING SERVICES

Service refers to work or advice sold to others. Buying a service is not like buying goods which may be touched and examined. When buying a service you must have confidence in the person performing the service. These people include tree surgeons, barbers, travel agents, doctors, painters, lawyers, cleaning women, movers, shoe repair men, roofers, and many others. Each year Americans spend about 40 percent of their income after taxes on services. It pays to shop as carefully for services as for goods. Before you buy services, compare prices and quality, and don't be afraid to ask questions. Who does the service? What does it include? What does it cost? Is satisfaction guaranteed? When you hire service people, remember the following:

1) Hire people you know or who are recommended.
2) Explain your needs clearly.
3) Discuss the work schedule.
4) Find out about parts, warranties, professional licenses, or academic degrees.
5) Work out the payment plan.
6) Find out how complaints may be handled.
7) If large sums of money are involved, be sure to get a contract. You may want a lawyer to look it over. His services are less expensive than a court's.

Most people never have been brought to court. Their business dealings are made with understanding on both sides. However, this is not always true. Tax matters, insurance problems, real estate transfers, contracts, or an accident, may incur lawsuit. When this happens you need to know your rights under the law. The services of professional legal minds may be required. This is expensive. The Bar Association usually sets guidelines for each kind of legal service. But lawyers' fees can differ. If you cannot afford a lawyer, consult the local Bar Association or the Legal Aid Society. These organizations may provide free professional services. The small claims court provides economical, prompt action on cases involving small sums of money, and you don't need a lawyer. But the best way to avoid legal bills is to avoid the causes of conflict by following the rules below:

1) Require people who perform services for you to get your specific consent for all tasks performed.
2) Read all wording in contracts carefully.
3) Get the exact meaning of all terms.
4) Obtain a copy of all contracts when you sign.
5) Consult a lawyer when you need legal service.

Education below the college level is available free in our country, but most education beyond high school is expensive. The average family expenditure for private education which often includes dancing lessons, music lessons, correspondence courses, books, and school tuitions is surprisingly high. As job standards go up, so does the demand for education. There are many private educational enterprises to meet the demand.

The pressure for stricter regulation of schools is growing. However, there are so many small businesses which require trainees that control is difficult. To ensure that the education you pay for is worth the money, look for professionals on the staff. Ask for the names and addresses of graduates and talk to them about the school. Make sure the school is accredited by a professional organization. To check the accreditation of a correspondence school, write to the National Home Study Council, 16 Eighteenth Street N.W., Washington, D.C. 20009.

If financial aid is needed, low cost school loans are available from many state and federal programs. Local professional organizations or unions often will give scholarships or loans if you meet their standards. Visit your guidance counselor, clergyman, or local library. Write also for the book, *A Guide to Student Assistance* from the Commissions on Labor, United States House of Representatives, Washington, D.C. 20036.

The most costly service you are likely to face is medical service. According to the federal Department of Health, Education and Welfare (HEW), the costs are now four times as high as they were twenty years ago. Each year the medical bill for each American averages over $324. For a family of five the bill would be $1,620, and the problem is getting worse. Despite this costly service, hospitals have been overrun with unnecessary cases. "We're simply a substitute for the family doctor," says the head of emergency service at New York's Roosevelt Hospital. A study by the United States Senate shows we should have 600,000 doctors. We have half as many. The governor of Texas recently reported that fifteen Texas counties have no doctors at all. Scarcity increases the cost of service in money and time.

The best key to low medical bills is to stay healthy. A study by the Massachusetts General Hospital showed that three of every five people could have stayed out of the hospital if they had consulted a doctor in time. Many were heavy smokers or were overweight; most were simply careless about their own health. Here are some guidelines to help you maintain good health:

1) Proper medical care through regular examinations, first-aid, and prompt treatment.
2) Good nutrition based on a proper daily diet.
3) Good dental care.
4) Physical activity selected to fit your needs and interest.
5) Satisfying work.
6) Healthy play and recreation.
7) Proper rest.
8) Safe play, travel, home, and work conditions.
9) Up-to-date family health record.

You should have a family doctor (general practitioner) who can get to know you. He should be the first person to see when your good health is threatened. Because he has your medical records, you can avoid expensive tests, re-tests, and delays. He can often give you advice over the telephone. You can discuss fees before he performs any services, and he should be able to help you curb medical costs. When necessary, he can refer you to the proper specialist or hospital, and he can save you money by recommending lower cost drugs. Usually he can give counsel on emotional problems as well. To find a qualified doctor or dentist call the local American Medical or Dental Association. Ask them to recommend a man or woman with a license to practice in your state. For your convenience your choice should be located close to you. To be certain you can get into a hospital, make sure your doctor is on the local hospital staff. Do not select a doctor unless you are able to trust him. If you become ill you must feel free to tell him everything about your illness. This sometimes may include something embarrassing. To tell him, you must trust him.

Having one regular dentist is nearly as necessary as having a regular doctor. At least 95 percent of Americans suffer from tooth decay at some time in their lives. Unlike bones or flesh the doctor treats, teeth cannot heal themselves; decay only gets worse. Regular six-month checkups are needed to prevent major problems which are painful, costly, and may result in loss of teeth. A balanced diet with plenty of crisp, crunchy vegetables and fruit is one of the best ways to avoid dental bills. Peanuts and popcorn are good too because they clean and exercise the gums and teeth. Soft, sticky, sugary, or starchy foods should generally be avoided. These form the acids that cause decay. Teeth should be brushed vigorously right after eating. Other guides to dental health may be obtained free from the American Dental Association, 211 East Chicago Avenue, Chicago, Illinois 60611.

The pharmacist in your drugstore is a licensed professional. He makes sure that all your medicine meets the official standards of strength and purity. Cut-rate or discount drugstores provide less expensive buys on drugs and vitamins. Since these must conform to government standards, you can save by making your purchases in these stores.

Ask your doctor to prescribe by the chemical name, not the brand name. The same company often makes an unknown less expensive brand which is just as effective. Never become a steady user of any drug, including aspirin. Your body is in a delicate balance which drugs are made to influence. Constant imbalance is dangerous. To be safe, follow these simple rules:

1) Ask the druggist to type the name of the drug on the label.
2) Take prescription drugs prepared only for you.
3) Read and follow directions for use.

4) Be cautious when using a drug for the first time.

5) Seek professional advice before combining drugs.

6) Seek your doctor's advice when symptoms persist or return.

7) Dispose of old prescription drugs.

8) Get medical checkups regularly.

The American Medical Association estimates that over $1 billion is wasted on useless "cures" yearly. If you are a victim, inform the FDA in Washington, D.C., or you local medical society. If the drug, device, or food was promoted through the mail, inform the post office. A color movie, *The Health Fraud Racket* is available rent free from the National Medical Audio-visual Center (Annex), Station K, Atlanta, Georgia 30334.

Most hospitals have all the equipment necessary to treat you properly for sickness, disease, or injuries. But this vital service is very expensive and is rising fast. Costs are figured on a day rate basis, usually about $100 a day. This includes general nursing care and meals. Your room, doctor's care, drugs, bandages, tests, X-rays, and special services are all added to the basic day rate. When you enter a hospital, you are asked to establish your credit. In emergency cases, credit is checked later. Clinics and wards provide reduced rate services. A doctor may be required to arrange your admittance. In many hospitals, you may be presented with the bill for partial payment before you leave. The expensive care for psychological and emotional problems may require even a more prompt payment. If you need low cost counseling for such problems write to: Family Service Association of America, 44 East 23rd Street, New York, New York 10010.

There are many ways to keep hospital costs low while getting medical attention. Use your community health services. Your public health department can tell you how to get free X-rays, vaccinations, and other low cost services. Public health nurses can give service in your own home at an hourly rate. Generally the fee is low and based on the patient's ability to pay. For more intensive care a nursing home may be needed. Obtain a recommendation from your doctor or local health department. Visit the home in person. If nursing homes are not satisfactory, try the *outpatient* department of the hospital. This is to provide hospital care to patients outside the hospital. They may have a plan that can meet your needs and budget. An outpatient visits the department regularly to be assured of constant treatment. A clinic or public health center can also provide outpatient services. These public and private agencies often provide their services free to those unable to pay.

If a long recovery period is required by your doctor, to avoid the exorbitant cost of hospitalization, ask if you can move to a *halfway house*. More and more hospitals have such a branch which is like a motel with a nurse. The cost is half the usual day rate. The community hospital is the least expensive for routine operations. The higher costs of the university or major city hospital might have to be paid if an unusual medical problem develops. Financial worries do not aid recovery. No service is a true service to you if it costs more than it is worth. However, good health is certainly worth the money needed to maintain it.

CHAPTER REVIEW

I. GAINING KNOWLEDGE

The following ideas are discussed in the chapter. Which of these facts are helpful to the consumer? Which are not? Be prepared to defend your answer.

1. The number of doctors in the United States is 600,000.
2. One billion dollars is spent on fraudulent cures each year.
3. The National Home Study Council checks schools.

II. BUILDING SKILLS

Each of the following is either a fact or an opinion. If it is a fact, there can be no argument against it. If it is an opinion, you can disagree and have your own view. Mark the statement F if it is a fact, and O if it is an opinion.

1. Lawyers charge too much.
2. Fifteen counties in Texas have no doctor.
3. A pharmacist prepares medicine.

A generalization is a statement or rule that groups together many facts. It includes many situations. The specific applies only to one definite situation and does not necessarily apply to other situations. Label the following statements as generalization (G) or specific (S).

1. Tree surgeons are professionals.
2. The Federal Government requires penicillin products to meet standards of purity.
3. Americans are the best fed people in the world.

III. EXPLORING VALUES

Do you agree or disagree with the following? Why?

1. Medical service is a right that should be provided to all Americans whether they can afford it or not.
2. Personal service sellers, such as barbers, should be allowed to limit the number of people entering their job

field. They should have the right to establish their own quality standards.

3. A woman who sells a cure for **baldness** (there is none) should be allowed to continue to service her happy customers.

IV. TAKING ACTION

Do one or more of the following.

1. For a list of nursing homes write: Joint Commission on Accreditation of Hospitals, 645 North Michigan Avenue, Chicago, Illinois 60611. Visit and compare.

2. To obtain a medical identification card write for an individual emergency information kit from: Emergency Identification—AMA, American Medical Association, 535 North Dearborn Street, Chicago, Illinois 60610.

   Such a card is recommended by the AMA for everyone but especially for those with health problems that may require special treatment such as:

   a) chronic health conditions that may cause emergencies,

   b) unfavorable reactions to medicines or materials commonly used in emergencies.

   c) unfavorable reactions when regularly used medicines are not continued at times when the person cannot communicate.

   d) inability to communicate.

3. For comparison find out the day rate charged at a local nursing home, halfway house, and local hospital. Find out the reasons for the differences in the rate.

4. For individual projects have each member of the class research a service he finds interesting. Each student should explore the range of prices for identical services. Discuss the reasons for the differences.

CHAPTER SEVEN
ADVERTISING

In our free market system, the buyer determines what will be sold. When he buys, he votes for the production of that good or service. The producer has the problem of trying to find out what will sell the best. In theory, he will try to develop the best product as quickly and as cheaply as he can. The better the job he does for the consumer, the higher his profit. However, he also faces the problem of mass market. He may want to sell to millions of people. Therefore, he may put millions of dollars into materials, employ thousands of workers, and produce tons of his new, lower-priced product. If no one knows it is superior, he will fail. The public will remain satisfied with the old, inferior product. So the producer informs the public of his product and creates a demand for it. He is competing against other producers for the dollar vote of the consumer.

The basic purpose of advertising remains socially useful. Advertising: 1) establishes and maintains reliable brand names and businesses; 2) promotes new improved products; 3) communicates new methods and uses; 4) encourages competition in quality, price, and service; 5) promotes worthy causes, such as charity, voting, health, and education campaigns; 6) pays for most of the mass communication in society: magazines, television, newspapers, radio; and

7) maintains continued sales, production, and employment.

Advertising has had some unexpected **effects upon** American life. Ads have tended to follow mass standards of taste. Far more creativity and cash go into ads than go into the articles of a **magazine. Ralph Nader** has blamed ads for the fact that "thousands of kids are growing up believing that **Pepsi** or Coke are necessary for a life of health and vigor." Automobile designs and advertising campaigns for years concentrated upon style rather than safety. The Federal Trade Commission has found that mass drug advertising has promoted drug abuse. Television advertising has enabled the big companies to completely take over entire fields. Only four soap companies sell 90 percent of all detergents used in the home.

The most expensive breakfast cereals are the most heavily advertised and reap the highest profit according to the National Commission on Food Marketing. Many have very low food value.

Advertising research has promoted scientific selling. For example, people prefer certain colors with different products, so artificial colors are added: blue for hardware, green for jewelry, pink for cosmetics. In many cases, the packages have become more important than the product. The *impulse* to make the purchase often replaces thought. According to *Women's Wear Daily,* a store continuously sold identical women's blouses in different packages for $3.95, $4.95, and $9.50. Each of the three blouses were successfully sold to the store's customers. The only difference was that some people were willing to pay more because they have a picture of themselves as being successful, sophisticated, and *au courant.* Advertising helps create this kind of image. In so doing, advertisements can have the power to change who we are. But the power to vote (buy) remains with us. The American consumer is becoming more aware of the power of advertising. It is no longer so easy to manipulate the successful, sophisticated consumer.

The chairman of the United States Senate's Commerce Committee says that deceptive selling is today's "most serious form of theft, accounting for more dollars lost each year than robbery, larceny, auto thefts, embezzlement and forgery combined." Most victims think they will get something for nothing. The product may be advertised as a brand name but may really only have a small part with the brand name. Many mail order firms are especially misleading in their descriptions and pictures. Even well-known newspapers and magazines carry misleading advertisements by questionable dealers.

Prices receive special attention. The *below wholesale* price appeals to many. According to *Consumer's Union,* no one sells below wholesale price; it is impossible to do so and remain in business. Typically the ad is used for the old bait and switch game. The customer is told the advertised item is out of stock or that something else is preferable. Then he is given a high pressure sales pitch to buy an over-priced item. Sometimes the price of the item advertised is misrepresented. The *wholesale price* suddenly is inflated by handling charges after the sale. Other ads for free merchandise are really based on the *pyramid club.* The buyer gets one item free if he sells the item to nine other people.

A variation is the *model service.* Your home with the sales item will be the ideal model for other customers. In return, the dealer will give you the item at the advertised wholesale price. The price is high or the product poor but the "deal" is made to sound good. No one comes to see the model, of course, and the salesman is already in the next town. Other advertisements stress the savings over the *reg-*

ular or *list* price. Sometimes a reputable newspaper or magazine will carry one brief advertisement for a product at an *inflated* price. Then the dealer advertises or says "as advertised in *Life* for $124.95, now $59.95." A variation is a coupon you clip out of an advertisement giving you "20 percent off the regular price." Another is the prize in a contest you did not enter. You must enter the dealer's place of business to claim the prize which turns out to be a so-called discount coupon to use for products he sells.

Some advertisements are effective although they do not deal with the characteristics of the product or its price. For example, some firms urge you to buy on the basis of charity. Many times only the promotor and salesmen receive any benefits, the charity never sees your money, while your support keeps the organization going. Trading stamps are another gimmick to save money. Usually the customer pays nearly 3 percent more for his purchases according to the Federal Trade Commission. When the stamps are exchanged, the products are valued at the highest retail prices. Today the trend is for retail stores to drop this "service" and lower prices. This final result is common for all gimmicks: give-away toys, glassware, tools, contests.

The Federal Trade Commission discovered that many advertising contests were deceptive. In a Capital Record Club contest, only 0.3 percent of its promised $4.5 million in prizes was awarded. In a Coca-Cola contest, thousands of $100 winners were disqualified by a secret rule. The F.T.C. now has rules that require all prizes to be awarded. The odds of winning must be made public. Of course, the higher costs of the fairer contests will be supported by higher prices. The product that is being promoted remains unchanged.

Advertising can be a very helpful guide in finding quality goods and services at a low price. To take advantage of advertising, you need to understand terms and phrases used. Some advertising terms are used repeatedly and have special meanings. It is helpful to know exactly what an advertisement is offering. Here are some of the most common:

1) *Sale:* Most of the items were bought specifically for this event. The greater number of items sold will result in lower prices.
2) *Clearance:* Goods which have not sold will be offered at lower prices to make room for new goods.
3) *Close-out:* The item will not be manufactured again and the dealer wishes to get rid of all the items he has.
4) *Reductions from regular, usual, or former prices:* The items did not sell well enough at these prices and thus lower prices are advertised. Frequently used in mid-season for clothes.
5) *Special purchase or comparable value:* The dealer has arranged a large order at a good price that he will pass on to you.
6) *Seconds:* The goods have defects that do not allow their sale as first class merchandise.

To use advertisements effectively you should look for factual information. Find the actual price, the size, the color, the material, the quality, the maker. Read over the terms of credit, trade-ins, trials, and guarantees. Find out how the product works and how it is serviced. Virginia Knauer, the President's assistant for consumer affairs, says advertisements for a product should "tell how it works and what it does. Housewives don't want to know if an appliance will make them sexier. They want to know. . .how long do they last? How easy are they to have serviced?" They also want the advertising writers to show they stand behind their claims by signing their names to their work.

You can handle your own complaints about goods and services by 1) trying to solve the problem with the seller, 2) writing to the company that made the product, and 3) sending carbon copies to local and state agencies, consumer groups, and the newspaper and radio. Your letter should be to the point and include all the important details. Copies, not originals, of important receipts or other papers should be included. However, the Better Business Bureau in New York City was swamped by 300,000 complaints in one year. The BBB is supported and operated by businessmen. In some cities they are not always able to protect the buyer against unfair business deals. Consumers can always turn to government agencies or seek legal assistance.

The government may be forced to act in order to preserve the free market system. Their job is 1) to guarantee a free choice to the consumer; 2) to preserve truth in packaging; 3) to prevent outright fraud; 4) to enforce minimum quality standards; and 5) to protect the health and safety of consumers. Recently Bess Meyerson Grant, Commissioner of New York City's Consumer Affairs, went to Times Square to enforce a city regulation that prohibited stores from advertising only the lowest price of an item. A large sign, "Microphones from $2.98," was found to be illegal. In addition the sign was taped to a microphone that cost $17.92. In Oklahoma, the state officer for consumer affairs helped a seventy-year-old woman with a monthly income of $180. She had unknowingly signed a contract for $10,000 worth of dancing lessons. She was released from her obligation. The studio had to stop making contracts with people obviously unable to benefit or pay. The Federal Government has curbed the attempt of television to influence thinking. Television commericals for cigarettes are forbidden. But the power of advertising to create ideas, to change behavior, to change the entire society, continues. Over $20 billion dollars are spent each year to promote this power. Each American can be exposed to as many as sixteen hundred ads a day! Smoking ads are probably the best example of the success of modern advertising. If advertising can be so abusive to humanity, what is it doing in our society?

CHAPTER REVIEW

I. GAINING KNOWLEDGE

Find the meaning of each of these words and phrases. Use each in a sentence of your own.

clearance	free market system
close-out	inflated
consumer	list price

II. BUILDING SKILLS

Each of the following is either a fact or an opinion. If it is a fact there can be no argument about it. If it is an opinion you can disagree with it and have your own opinion. On a separate sheet of paper mark each statement F if it is a fact, O if it is an opinion, and N if you are not sure.

1. People pay for merchandise that is over-priced.
2. Tricking a buyer is worse than stealing.
3. Those who sign without reading deserve to be cheated.
4. Misleading advertisers risk breaking the law.

III. EXPLORING VALUES

Do you agree or disagree with the following? Why?

1. Some people think there should be one government selected brand for most products. They believe this would save money.
2. Life would be better without any advertising or it should just promote worthwhile causes.
3. In effect the post office laws give federal tax money to advertisers. They are allowed to send mail to customers below the cost of delivery. This practice should not be allowed.

IV. TAKING ACTION

Do one or more of the following.

1. Clip advertisements from the local newspaper. Compare

the features of effective advertisements with those of poor ads. Point out which are the most useful to the consumer. Share your findings with your class.

2. Contact your local radio station and newspaper. Ask them how they regulate advertising. How much do they depend on advertising money to operate?

3. Invite an advertising man to class. Ask him to explain how an advertising campaign is conducted.

4. Make two separate lists, one headed "Consumer Services Performed by Advertising," the other "Harmful Effects of Advertising." Compare the lists.